The Dream We Call Reality

The Dream We Call Reality

Forty Days and Nights in the Fire

LUFUNO ROMEO MANWADU

RESOURCE *Publications* · Eugene, Oregon

THE DREAM WE CALL REALITY
Forty Days and Nights in the Fire

Resource Publications
An Imprint of Wipf and Stock Publishers
199 W. 8th Ave., Suite 3
Eugene, OR 97401

www.wipfandstock.com

PAPERBACK ISBN: 979-8-3852-4911-4
HARDCOVER ISBN: 979-8-3852-4912-1
EBOOK ISBN: 979-8-3852-4913-8

VERSION NUMBER 102925

Contents

Outro

Preface

THIS COLLECTION, THE DREAM We Call Reality, is the fruit of years apart drawn from different moments and seasons-- of recurring revelations, visions and poetic reflections under spiritual longing and personal wilderness since childhood. of all the hundreds of other poems that throughout years got lost, missing or destroyed, this collection stands as a concise reclamation and resurrection of all that was lost. These 40 poems, chosen to correspond with the 40 days and nights of Jesus in the wilderness, are an offering not only of words but of worship—in awakening from this dream we call "Reality." These poems are not merely for the ear, but for the heart. They speak of solitude, fire, and the loudness of the so called "still small voice of God" in the desert. They walk between the old and the new, the mystic and the flesh—leading us to repent. The five outro poems are to correspond with the number 5 which is symbolic to Gods grace, mercy and favor-- meant by the writer to stand for any pieces amongst the 40 that may not resonate or be as valuable to each unique reader, to make sure each reader is covered with their total of a valuable 40 pieces or even more at the end.

1.

The dream we call reality

In this rhythmic spinning wheel—
Seeming real just to weigh the human will—
A speck in the vast cosmic sea,
That hums on the key of C, as it spins,
Thoughts shifts across awareness frequencies.
Yet we feel steady—shifting feet's—
Across tides of victories and defeat.
Blindfolded we lough and sing,
Not knowing we are dancing towards a stinging thing.
In this world we are living in,
The conclusions we make on a human reasoning;
In oblivion the things we be believing in;
The confusions we make,
Around the big bang and the biblical beginning.
Unless we succumb to the mass awakening,
Eventually to see heavenly—what's really happening;
From this reality—dream,
Where blinded by what the eye can see,
We fail to heed the actual battle
Unsettled between the two extremes:
The kingdom within, and a life of seamless sin,
As the poles unseen, we polarise between.

It's time indeed, to wake up—
To seek, to climb the ladder of Jacob,
And to fill to the brim the sacred cup,
Before earth in robes of wrath can quake up
Just to wake us.

It's time the veil gets torn,
For the souls reform.
The spirit awakes and pride is gone,
When one can truly see —

the dream we call reality—
Empty in promises.

Riches and materiality are not what they claim to be,
When the monitor alarm comes to beep.
Only God can bless with eternal bliss.
Under systems insincere that seem to be;
And lucrative schemes with no good to bring—
We be pleasure trap targets
Yet in ignorance
we see the world as a subject—
to our fleshly urges—
based on the worth of assets,
and all we can and can't afford,
in no accord with the word of God—
As the tinier route we dodge
to the pit unfit.
With gifts of the creators hand sinfully spent;
Neglected sense, and wasted chance;
True prophet's principles bent,
and lacking lessons learnt;
Temples of the holly ghost turned
to tents of pretence.
We live as though we're just the flesh—
Breaking the temple before we go to church;
In false embrace of the inner-self we forget even just to stretch;
Losing cotton and linen we dress on fabrics nearly dead;
Junk fed— some say if you know the risen king—
No need to believe in him,
some say he lives in us some say we live in him.
Some claim to know the truth, some just live it.
We detach from nature,
and chase the man-made;
Against the scripture pray
in public attention—voice raised;

Failing to chase divine fate if we get paid—
Giving to what the flesh crave—
In forgetting this are the last days.
Sometimes I ask myself—
If I chose to come to earth,
On this race this time and space;
At times I feel — I do not fit—
Like spirit too grand for this earthly kit—
I feel like light that cannot be caged;
Like I've been here before the Ice age—
That I existed eons before the birth—
Before the first foot stepped on earth
I feel like I'm everywhere I see—
One with the sun and the sea.

2.

Fear not (oracle poem)

If you are down to earth,
fear not to be ashamed.
If you subdue the flesh,
fear not a binding chain.
If your sins are confessed—
You get another chance—
to seek the kingdom first;
If you live content
the lord shall quench your thirst.

If you really repent
you shall find your heaven on earth.
If you say never again
to the vices of yesterday,
heaven is yours to stay.
If you played your part,
and to the cross your sins you cast—
fear no flames of hell,
against your past.

If you grow a giving hand, fear no lack;
on season you reap no less—than your deserved share-
elsewhere in one way or another as just and fair.
If you tell your truth, and stick to your word—
fear not to be misled—
the Lord shall guide your steps.
If you take not what is not yours—
by unfair force, fear no loss;
all that was taken from you was not lost,
all you lost was not really yours.

If you do all you can, with just what you have,
ahead lays the prizes you deserve.

If you seek first to serve—
fear no starvation.
If you abide by the word—
fear no temptations.
If you contaminate not the temple—
there shall be no more starvation
for the soul but yours is salvation.
If you never lose your regrets and pain,
Transmuting them to triggers some change—
Broken are the chains
of regret and shame,
that constrains.
If you are not guilty,
fear no false blames—
the Lord is your witness.
If you harm no fellow sentient beings in vein,
feel safe from God's loin's chase.
If you walk with God—
fear not to be alone;
If the lord knows your tone—
fear not to be unknown,
by the world.
If you drink the living water—
fear no might of thirst,
If you tame your tongue—upset,
You now can pass the test.

3.

The property of the supreme

I am the property,
Of the supreme—
The palm, of the creator's hand.
Along the deserts
I'm a spring,
Of quench that never ends.
To serve—I'm one of the sent, with a plan—
To fix the concerns of a thousand clans.
Through me broken hearts are mended;
When it's dark, I'm the lamp
The LORD recommended.
Since I ascended,
I remain unbranded-
To cynics and snobs—uncomprehended.

I synchronise with the speed of the planet's spins,
And grasp the language of trees;
By the sea I listen to the sound of the wind, as it sings
Away the planet's sins.
I'm the voice of caution—
Devoted to divine devotions.
To mend the hearts broken—
I speak with the moons emotion,
Foes—I bring close with heart open.
I'm the mouth of the enslaved,
And the brunch of the brave;
Advised by the wise, of the skies—
A divine device,
Fitted with foresight,
And a stand by fuel tank for the flight.

4.

I made a promise

I made a promise—
And I'm trusted for my task;
to accomplish and to leave the tools intact,
Before ascension, with a new past—
to the courts, where we account.
I made a promise,
Before I was armed and deployed—
That my existence won't be void—
In the land I will serve,
With just what I have.

I made a promise—
That I'll pass this test.
Before I came to earth—
Accepting birth,
To find my value and worth;
And to bow below the heavenly wrath.
Will the world makes me forget,
My promise and the purpose
For which I was meant.

I made a promise
To pay off my karmic debts
And to play my part;
To live in truth and to speak my heart.
I made a promise to face my fears and doubts;
To embrace the trip,
And to let my heart speak to its peak,
To the last clock's tick.

5.

I just wanna live right

After all my wrongs I just wanna live right.
I just wanna speak life,
and learn the law to live wise,
in Gods eyes.
I just wanna give thanks for life before each sunrise;
keep to my truth and shun lies;
I just wanna carry the cross,
to let the Christ inside
decide my strides.

With this lifespan—
I just wanna be in line with Gods plan;
I just wanna rise above my vices—
live grounded to take advices
without a judgment.
I just wanna take advantage
of every opportunity presented,
to be a better vessel for the gospel.
Lord I need your intervention—
above material possessions,
give me a heart to seek salvation.

I just wanna find my divine worth
and stick to Christ's words—
to close the gap
between what I know and the works of my own hands.
I just wanna be humble to the young and old—
as time unfolds—
of the word—to take heed and grab hold;
By the Torah—to do just as told.

6.

Make me your servant (Devotional poem)

My highly reverent!
say to me just a sentence,
to turn my heart tender and repentant;
Save me from a smooth tongue of a serpent,
and make me your servant.
Draw me close to your presence,
and make me your permanent patient—
lest I stay a vulnerable target
to the plans of the savage.
Of my defects—
they take advantage.
On my vices—
they give no advices.

Come save me from this box
in which I'm thinking.
In the lake of lowly thoughts,
my boat is quickly sinking;
I'm a slave to the savage systems—
compliant to canal kingdoms.
On my strengths I stay defeated;
dragged to submission,
and drained to depletion,
lost on a mission—
behind the bars
of mental prisons—
people pleasing.

Foes that tries to track me,
won't find me if I'm in your safety.
My vessel is empty, and my soul is thirsty—searching,
for a path apart from the streets that strays me.
If I fail, do not forsake me;

Let no troubles overtake me,
but let the pain come
that trains me.
Hear me in my calling,
catch me in my fallings,
and let yours be
the glory.

7.

Where can a man hide

Do you see me with such sight
as that of a man's eyes—
down here from a bird eyesight—
and stay at the blue skies,
heaven as your right hand side?
or you reside right inside
the temple, where from you no man can hide.
Can your steady gaze be dodged like a finite man's kind—
that without the light seeks yet never finds,
ever blind to what's too far or behind?

Upon your throne, in your full charge,
do you err like a human judge does?
Do you watch without keeping us
under your mighty guards?
Do you rebuke every trespass
with no regard for integrity's rewards?
For you to see is the setting sun alone in charge;
Can any being trick your sight,
that sees atoms heartbeats—
O! most high?
If your eye whirls with every rushing gust,
ever cast at every spark of dancing dust,
in the guard of the just,
where then can a man hide?
If you foresee man and his off springs;
Hearing the chords of his heartstrings-
his tears uncried and the songs his cells sings,
can anything stand between?
If you witness my nightly dreams;
and the rhythm of sun rays hymns;
Roaming every realm as God Elohim.

If your eye is ever cast
at every angle of every dimension,
of present, future, and past;
Beyond acted expressions,
and first impressions misconceptions lust—
In mid night's gloom or under the sunlight alike
despite the pace in motion or size—
of the thing on sight.
Through the stars as they shine
and through the birds of the sky,
If you keeps an open eye.
all stashes remains on the spotlight,
to your most high eye.

8.

Pranked by the LORD

You are alone
pranked by the LORD,
through the world, with all it holds:
Pure diamonds and glitters like gold.
When the blindfold is off,
you are alone in the ring—
all your back and fourth
and the courage song you sing,
with all your strength and sweat —
all you fight is yourself.

You are alone—
it is only yourself you oppose.
Your manifestations,
are just your thoughts and words
exposed;
All misfortunes are burdens
Self-imposed.
All you see as apart reflects yourself—
on the mirror you hold;
under trials, day and night, stars beholds your routes,
and the ground on which your heart takes roots.
You are alone prone to surprise,
your task is just to rise to your prize,
or descend to the curse—
facing this test.
Bad and good angels would like to see,
how much you can repent,
given this chance.

9.

Ill show you more things you can do

Some land, some trees
Filled with a righteous glee,
To a dancing degree—
They blossom with attitude—
In gratitude—
bearing their fruits in abundance—
In show off to providence.
They say: "look what more we can be,
We were content just to be and to breath.
Then God replies:
" May you live on and multiply,
Behold it is just the beginning, note it down,
I'll show you more that you can be;
You shall find that you are not apart—
But a part of the moon and the sea;
It shall be evident
that you are just a hand—
providence extends."

Some birds puts art in flight
each time
they realise they remain on the sportlight—
to the ever gazing eye.
They start singing:
"You are a crafty creator most high—
Indeed you are unmatched in skill;
Only destruction reigns against your will;
Your light transcends the sunshine.
Those who attempt to compete with you—mighty one,
returns to seek your help in trembling and tears.
Who can rise to your perfection o lord, in all of your creation.
Look what we can do beneath the blue—

as a proud work
of your crafty hands.
Look how high we fly in style "
Then the Lord replied:
"Behold I'll show you more things to testify—
You shall know the truth,
that when to nature you are turned—
you are the vessel I be living through.

10.

You know me not (oracle poem)

You expect me to come from amongst the stars—
Yet I'm part of who you are.
In heart you suppose—I have a blindness,
Mistaking my kindness, for a weakness.
You catch me not,
On the frequency your mind is turned in to.
I'm right before you, yet you hope to see me soon;
You preach my omniscience
Yet you tell me the things you are going through;
You know not the origin of the knowledge in schools.
I'm your God yet on my throne—you place the "books of truth—"
Deafening your ear, as I speaks directly to you,
And making nature a fool,
With the kind of foods you choose.

Within you search not,
Only from the skies, you expect me to descend,
Only in despair to my voice—unturned you attempt to attend
In your ignorance and pride, to know me—you pretend,
But where can the cruel come across me,
If not in the harvest of their sowing hand,
Is there a piece of land?
When shall the dishonest finally find me,
If not in the effect of their own cause;
Is there a certain spot?
You know me not,
I'm here but still you wait
For me to come.
You know me not, you hold a far-fetched faith—
Doubting me in every trouble you come to face.
In hiding from me,
Still you think you're safe.

11.

The still voice

Turn the knobs
of your mental tools,
from radio static, to nature's tune—
Immersed in to the celestial school.
On its eternal shift the still voice never cheats;
Its chores it never shirk,
To serve who ever seeks,
With speech sweet—free of deceit—
what symbols conceals—it speaks
you need not go outside to seek,
the still voice never goes to sleep,
No offs days no leave
Forms to fill;
Yet we clog the ear within
With the flesh we're in,
As it falls to sin.
Only to deem it a tiny thing,
in the loudness of lower frequencies
being intense, in itself.
when we get the sixth sense intact.
Meek and still—it never screams or rise extreme,
neither will it dare retreat,
to serve below our Godly needs,
if we take no heed.
hence as further we stray,
the tinier it seem to be,
as more hazier we start to see.
towards a graceless pit.

12.

The super conscious state

When I think of God I picture no more
The painting of Adam's creation,
But love expressed in all spheres dimensions—
The manifestation of nature's good intentions.
I won't build a tower
Like Babel—
To reach the heavens.
I may refer to God as he or she
Yet in my mind there is no man or woman I see.
I do not hold in mind a God with a human face—
Dressed on a certain race,
But the super conscious state—
Through which all things came to place;
Expressed throughout nature;
Seasons as its loving traits—
Mother Nature,
With whom we are co-creators,
and originators.
When to God—I call
I call upon the reason and the cause of existence—
Beyond "efficient"—
Unbound by time or distance in persistence.—
The self-sufficient without external assistance.
When I say "God"
I mean the force behind
all of nature's course—
As megaannums passes and rocks forms,
and through earth's veins—as rivers flow;
I mean the fuel to the inter galactic motions;
In heart the highest emotion;
Fair and kind
behind every specie

science is yet to find—
of the skies and below the generous ground.
The one who lights the sun
and let us freely breathe;
as though we never breach—
The inspector
of intentions behind deeds,
and true needs beyond human greed—
whose hands are fruit bearing trees,
giving in season— seasoning free.

13.

Behind the scenes

Who tells planets to spin,
And light the stars to shine.
In nature so divine,
Who composed the songs birds sings.
Which mind designed
Patterns on butterflies' wings.
Beyond the space and time—
Whose light outshines the sun.
Whose wrath—in a breath
Causes the earth to quake;
Whose math sets
the globes in shape?
Which artist sang
existence into place?
Who sets the laws that operates,
Impossible to break.
Upon the throne the ruler worthy of praise.
Who causes every hand that sows, to reap—
Speaking through both thunders and human lips;
To be blessed whose word do we have to keep;
Birds—who gave them wings to fly
Through the open sky.

14.

Desire (allegorical fiction poem)

Long before the beginning,
before the birth of dawning and evenings
and before the atomic seedling of the milky ways.
Long before time and space;
before there was void in place,
and before formlessness could be traced.
Long before the numbering of days—
Before earth and human race,
there was Desire—the light, and the fire—
unfelt untapped all satisfied in itself.
There was nothing for desire to aspire
External of itself, it was self-inspired;
and apart from desire—nothing could be.
There was nothing desire could hear,
for all sound was glorious music
perfectly harmonious in itself.
There was nothing to be expressed
outside of "Desire—the light and the fire"
for it was full expression in all patterns and forms,
all skill and all the art abundant within it—unseen.
being all parts of all things,
Nothing was impossible—for the thought was the fire
and everything desired would instantly materialize,
yet desire was one and perfect in itself— unrealised,
not possessed by any realm's being.
In desire was all that could make and all that could be made.
Until it desired time,
and there was suddenly a point of time,
when desire was unsatisfied
in itself as all there was.
Suddenly there was space—desired could fill,
as all living things.

Every plant that brazenly springs
and every bird that sings;
Every far star,
and every little deep sea.

15.

Live out of love

Let love reign— guiding you,
to your rightful devotions.
Silence the ocean of counter emotions—
To let love pace your motion;
Keeping intact your golden intentions,
and the motives behind your actions.

Let love fit you on other peoples shoes;
Amongst those against you—
In heart find no foe.
Serving from your heart, not to earn
For your terms or to prove.

Preserve love in your heart—
To walk in line with nature's intentions:
This is to let God live through you as a person.
Let love guide your inter-actions,
Against reactive-transgressions.

What makes a person loving?
Find and treasure that thing
Then you got wings,
To lift to pastures—heavenly green.
For once love is stolen from your heart strings,
The heart plays but no bird along sings.

16.

How far can your love go

From the strength of love—
how much can you let go,
of the treasures of the world and let God.
In exchange—how much value does your love hold.
Through blazing fires—
is it withered grass or pure gold?
If God is love—
is the flame in your heart the same God?
Through tempests of spring—
Does it stand bold;
Or soon like dust—
away its all blown.
After stumbling blocks and hush storms—
is it a love that stays strong;
Is it pretentious or—a love sure;
Smeared with lust or—white pure;
How far can your love go?
Is it deaf to nay sayings;
Leaving mistakes space—
Burning innocent
stronger than thirst,
In the chest?

17.

A place of no pardon

After the lessons unlearnt;
And a thousand failed tests;
And after the last second chance
have long—past.
Widely opens the giant cruel gates—
Ready to swallow into the starving belly
Of the scorching ground.
Where thundering blazes
Makes deafening sounds
In a place of no pardon,
For the uncast—burdens,
And every heart—hardened,
Where they scream:
"One more chance! One more chance!
And I will never be the same again".
Intense diameter of the jingling bonding chains.
In millenniums of burning droughts,
With no drizzling rain.
Living in the blinding gloom with no
Form and no name.

In a place of no pardon
Where from a distance
We hear lamentations for assistance:
"One more chance! One more chance!
And I will never be the same again!"
In the pit of loss and shame;
Toxic gases and random flames.
With no sun and no rain
in burning thirst, and shallow breath
Under the unrest of the divine wrath,

Where in pain
One asks for death,
In vein.

18.

The trap of guilt

I see you are still held in the shells
Of your past mistakes;
With the grudge you hold against yourself—
Your heart inflates.
By the look on your face, one can see—
Though you are free, you still don't flee
The slavery cage.
Now free yourself from the chains of shame
Cleansed in The name you are not the same,
You are made new, within the very frame—
Thinking you are still caught
In the trap you escaped;
Prone to the aches of past mistakes—
Your grief leads to big falls,
Predators knows your pitfalls.
To moan turned—your inner chore;
Shame was the mentor,
Self-captured—
The cage—you did enter.

19.

By the end of the tunnel

Never give up,
through thorny roads.
When fears pitch up—
keep the faith you hold.
Through lessons life teach us—
just keep up.
Never throw the towel,
by the length of the travel.
There is a waiting sunlight,
by the end of the tunnel;
Golden routes—by the end of the gravel;
Time for the harvest;
After the times that are hardest.
It is the route less taken,
that leads to the heavens.
Fear and doubt—
Peaks when victory is about.

20.

After the rain

Rise again after the fall,
be sure to be better than before,
in what you sow.
Like an angel deployed
With a double edged sword—
In the fire bring the fourth,
Humble in thoughts—
Patient on your pace.
Begin again after the rain
and tough terrains.
No ticking goes to waste
Without a forced haste.
Could you complete the course
Applying the entire force
from the take off?

21.

we could

We could have been better,
Or even worse;
We could have been gentler—
So to sin less.
We could have avoided the trouble,
That was seamless.
We could have reaped in double,
With all our needs met.
We could have not rebelled,
But learnt to love maths,
We could have been stronger,
As a planet to avoid the whole mess.
We could have walked wiser,
To grasp the second chance with both hands,
In converse of transgressed precepts.
We could have seen further,
Through the spirit sense.
Had we been honest—
We would have found rest
Inside the Lord's nest.
Still around earth—
Perhaps sent to serve somewhere else.
We could have opened new doors,
By leaning to let go.
We could have learnt early to say No
to lacking laws, and worldly wars.
Had we pardoned our debtors—
We could have paid off our karmic debts,
Had we dwelt upon the proverbs—
Better we could have dreamt—
Spared from what we dread.
Had we taken Jesus' own words:

Matthew's chapters—five to seven—
We would have seen the earthly heaven.
Deeper had we went, within ourselves—
We could have found what the scriptures really meant,
And more that cannot be taught or learnt.
Had we done all we could, with just what we had,
Honoring both the Sabbath and Lent
We could have been far ahead,
with our prayers heard.

22.

From today on

From today on
The former is all gone.
I'm taking off the old gown—
learning to let go;
to take off, and never stop;
Mountains—to climb, rivers—to cross.
Away from a zone of comfort

With lessons from past mistakes;
It's time to build over from scratch;
Time to start over again,
Before more time is wasted
Into the blaming game;
Time to move on
And to let go
Of the dragging shame.
No more basking
On past loses and victories,
No more holding on
To horrors of history.

From today on
I leave the past behind
And chose to keep in mind
That life has no rewind,
What can change—
Be all I mind.

23.

If you are not in charge (Devotional poem)

If you are not my shield,
I have no place to run to;
If you won't defend me
I shall not win the battle.
If you are not on my side,
I know I'm on the wrong side.
If you were not the fair judge,
I would even be terrified to be alive.
If you were not in charge
How would life be fair;
If you are not my God;
I'm ruled by the spirit of death.
If I transgress
Nothing can defend me
Against your wrath.
If I'm not sent by you, all my works
are childish,
And ready to reach the ditch
with other waste.
Without your lead my fruit is without
taste or nutrition.
You gently guide men,
Through conscience and intuition.
Apart from you is terror and confusions.
I will run to you oh lord,
Before my sins start chasing me.
You know how less I know oh lord
So I will abide by the golden rule.
I shall seek for a shield in your guarding principles.
You hide from me what I won't handle—
most merciful.
Your light is not of a candle;

For all actions you see the root intentions,
Guide me o lord to your true perfections.

24.

Your righteousness shall rise

Like that of a chastising Christian
or a Muslim,
on the Ramadan month—God pleasing;
Like a Rastafarian who finds a rightful reason
to go vegan;
Let your walks be like that of a monk
or a nun.
Taking blames,
Judging none—blaming none.
Despite fraternities loving all—
People of diversity as though they are only one.
You shall be on time
Like earth orbits the sun,
And strait to the point
Like a bullet from a gun—
When it's done.
Like The Son
You shall reach the state to say "forgive them for they know not
what they do"
Your righteousness shall surpass that of gentiles and Jews;
And some of the scribes who wrote the holly books.
In everything you do, you shall not lean on your own point of
views.
You shall live like those who went to glimpsed hell
And sent back, on a last chance.
Now more diligent in all the works of your own hands,
You shall live like you finally found the last chance—
You long searched.
Like a farmer who sows as they would like to reap.
You shall dwell in the safety of the law you keep.

25.

Humble yourself

Humble yourself
to the tiniest insect—
In your footsteps—
Adhering to all set precepts—
Humble yourself
in all your earthly works,
When no one inspects.
Humble yourself to mother earth
be satisfied with the only bunch she bares;
Humble yourself to the atoms of your cells;
Taming the mouth—extend the inner ear.
Seek no much respect and material worth
to keep, below the godly wrath.

26.

Nature's brand

Your heart is no hand
to hold a grudge;
Your body is no temple
to party inside.
Your mind is no villain's Dan;
Your passion is no idle burn—
It seeks divine expression.
Do not remove the logo—
You are nature's brand.
Shut your ears
Against the world and groove
To the jams
of the inner band.

27.

True worship

What noble thing can we do,
Is there anything of glory
in Gods point of view—
by human strength and intellect;
Is there any wisdom or extent of talent;
Is there anything that can be leant;
Is there anything of true worth—
than the remembrance of the self—
each was meant to be at first;
Is there anything we can do,
Than subdue our lusts and basal moods—
Attuned to the realm of truth.
Is it not what true worship is—
When we let nature take its course,
Without standing on its way—
For the One in us to lead the way.
When attuned to nature
Is it not glory
To the dweller of the temple;
Embracing natures order and art,
And feeding only from nature's supply—
Is this not how we testify,
Of the power with which we identify;
Observe the birds sing and fly
And give praise to the most high;
Stare at the stars of the night sky
And embrace the gift of life—
Living not as we like
But in self-sacrifice
And being set apart;
With a willing soul,
In the depth of heart;

Feeding clean the dwelling temple of the majesty;
At last to ever be dressed modestly—
and keeping all our promises—
is this not what the recipe
For true worship is:

To do all we can—
To see materialize
The higher plan.

28.

Upon the crucifix

Some artists imagine a human face
That despite race—
Would resemble the law—
Just to draw the lord.
Some drew him hair hanging loose.
Some covered with a doek,
They dispute as though it was about the looks.
Yet in truth some of the paintings mocks
Unfit- for holly books.
Now let's see the humble artist—
Who paints in love and truth
They dispute on his race,
As though there was more need
To see his actual face,
Than hear each word he had to say;
To let him lead the way.
If you make your way to the market place,
You may not know which of his painting to pick.
Amongst those portrayed—with meanings that contradicts.
Before you know it:
There is another painting of his
Trending in the streets,
Not as humble and meek—
With an earring and a wink.
There are no words any of them speak;
They have no thousand words to paint,
Yet on saints walls they lay fixed
With him nailed on an upright stick,
Without a cross on the crucifix—
Than letting ours be—
To practice the word he had to preach.

29.

Why are we here

After the Godly ways;
after the gloomy days—
the high and by ways,
and after the last days;
Why are we here
at first place—
remains the constant quest.
If we came to start afresh in the flesh
or to fix some karmic debts,
Or just under eternities test.
Being spirit why body and soul,
as fragmented parts of the whole.
After each one's role,
what destiny—is the main goal.
Through gusts, heats and colds;
Base stone, and gold;
More stars and globes.
Why are we here—
Each clothed on a certain race
Loved and so dear
with assigned number of days.
Why hope and despair;
under the service of the same sun
where the laws to which we should adhere
can be summed up to just one.
Why such operations so fair;
Beauties unique beyond compare
What message does each spare.
after it's all done,
what is the primal plan
Of this planet shared
within a given lifespan.

What point is there,
in finding purpose and peace,
Walking bare feet and hugging trees.
After we are back to spring,
and after all that life is yet to bring,
to God is there still a surprising thing?

30.

The only map

Of all the floods of mind,
just a millilitre, is required.
the mass of seas—unkind
are for none to enquire,
If you try to look beyond the sky,
all you see is blue.
You need not construe—
Everything—true—
Just what God wants you to do,
gets you through.

31.

Devine direction (prayer poem)

When foes are before me;
When they mock and scorn me,
When it's too dark and stormy;
to see where I'm going,
Turn your light and show me
Where I'm stepping surely;
Guide me to my calling,
lest I keep conforming,
in the shade of folly

Cause my inner eye to see,
a thing for what it is—
To dissect the facts from fantasies.
Say your word, and show me a sign;
Tell me I'm your art work—your hand design;
Give me a mandate, and show me the task—
to which I'm assigned.

32.

The inner light

If I dare to ask the Lord,
He answers not
With a thunderous rod—
Sometimes through those who asked before—
the silent sage's wisdom's stores.
So I bow low to knowledge high,
To voices past I don't deny.

I read their views—i test their claims—
Not every fire is holy flame.
But in the pages truth may hide,
If read with open heart and mind.
I find the false, embrace the right,
through the inner light.

33.

Trust the most high

When robbed and betrayed—
Trapped and led astray
After all is purely judged and weighed—
You shall finally find your way.
At the end of the day
Everything taken from your tray
Shall return multiplied.
All your foes shall flutter like sparrows—terrified.
On their schemes to impede
The rightful reaping of your sowing—
They shall lose against the divine.
When they confront your views and faith
And wish for your plans to fail—
Don't you bow and bend your tale—
Trust the law—
You won't be led to shame.

When people change
all of a sudden;
When they pray to see
you broken hearted with hatred—
Cease not to tender your inner garden, regardless—of the Godless
For you are none of their subjects,
and from your garden alone,
you are to be provided.

When the world tries to break you down.
When your toils turns into their laughing stock
When they mock and make you the clown,
Don't you let it turn your mind,
from blessing thoughts or make you frown;

When their hearts grow canal—

Incapable of carrying compassion.
When they despise your progress,
and plan for you to transgress,
Stick to the right verse.
When to your good deeds
they keep a blind eye,
trust the most high
whose scales in judgement—
cannot lie

34.

I can see

I'll prevail, I'll be free;
When critics lie—I will flee;
When rivers dry—I'm the sea;
Before troubles come—I'll foresee
When the opponent prompts a retreat,
With eyes fixed upon the crucifix—
Thoughts of defeat I resist.

I'm like a tree
Whose roots sips from living streams—plenty with figs.
Deep down I'm only fulfilled when I feed those in need.
Now that I can see,
When dross glitters and appeals-
In lack, still I won't steal a thing.
Prone to rage and grief, I'll be still.

In mental prisons you can sentence me,
But still I trust "Him" who strengthens me
Against all that threatens me.
There is always escape
From the villain's hands—
A room for a second chance
If we repent.
Above tales words can tell—
That letters can spell;
If internally—I burn and to truth—I turn,
Than my past—I can rise times ten.

35.

Why should I not bless you(Oracle poem)

If you are not intending to harm
your fellow beings,
or to shake hands in forbidden deals—
Driven by fairness and honesty—
If you stick to all your promises—
Staying a blessing to my people—
Humble to both the wise and simple;
If you admit your flaws—
repent and abide by the Law,
then victory is yours.
If generously you sow—
why should you not harvest for your sowing.
If you remember me when you rise—
why should I not pick you when you are falling.
When your heart says I'm sorry—
I'm your God I get your story;
I can't stop my glory from pouring—
as to my law you keep conforming.
If I'm familiar to your tone—
Will I not recall when you call?
If you walk in righteousness—
Why should your fate be Sheol?
If you mind what feeds your soul —
Why would heaven not be your home?
In despair let me be your hope,
If you keep this tiny route.

36.

By the oases

From the thrones spared—
One may just stare
As time less cares—
Not knowing what is not fair;
Merry yet we much err.
Pity how we chase air;
With eyes wide—
To stand and just stir
Expecting the sunrise
From the setting west.
Stashing a rightful request—
By the oasis—dying of thirst—
In heaven treated like guests—
As royal clans in rustic shacks.
When truth twisted—
Upon your freedom
The foe feasted.

37.

The knowledge of the Godly truth

No diamond in the ground—
Lies too far to be found.
No mountain is too gentle to climb—
It is just a matter of plan and time
No worthy truth can hide
If we search inside.
No stronghold is too strong to stay—if you cast "this kind."
No goal is too far to meet;
No day earth spins too fast—to send a silent wish.
No vices cannot be refrained;
No mental slave cannot be unchained;
No good is too good to be true—
With the knowledge of "the Godly truth."
If we persist along the cliffs,
And deem each thought of doubt a thief,
As we think—to see thoughts as seeds;
That sprouts to plants
From which we feed.

38.

When gold lays just three fits

To quit or to still persist—
To cease to dig furtherer the pit,
Or to resist defeat.
To quit, as such to break the deal,
To numb the primal zeal,
And so by loss of hope and will.
When gold lays just three fits,
To quit, or to still persist,
Remains the puzzling trick;

Despite a stumble of feet, to still persist,
Or to quit—the vows to fail to keep.
To deem yourself unfit, or to resist defeat.
Which yoke do you pick;
To break or to stick
To the words
you speak?

39.

Somewhere along the trail

As we persist in pursuits
of canal comforts
and briefed treasures of the world,
Is the end not sorrow—that unfolds?
In holly service if we hold on—
Through hardships and pain—
Is peace of mind not to be attained.
To truly succeed—
Is there no slight struggle that precedes?
does the pleasures we seek,
over peace—not impede
the channel to receive,
what has already been bought—
Waiting for the heart to believe?

Run on
There is a single threshold step
Into new strength
Somewhere along the trail—
Where no fatigue prevails.
At the end of the day—
Is the sweetness of sugar
not the pleasure to ills;
And the bitterness of herbs
not the torture that heals.

40.

By the dusk

When my life comes to an end—
Before the captains
What will I present—
When there are no more curtains,
Over what nature intends—
When I can no longer change or pretend
When there is no more resisting sin
Or fighting temptations—
Will I not blame what I've been facing—
in testing.
Will my soul be forsaken?
Back to the whole will my spirit be taken?
On the task for which I was sent—
The promise—will I have kept.
When there have come a turn—
to eternity to make a turn—,
at the end,
as the flesh breaks down to sand—
what will I have planted upon the land.
Will there be a chance
To be told what I failed to understand.

What lessons will I have learnt?

Will there still be a chance
to repent without the flesh with which I go through tests.
Will I be born again on earth—
to start afresh.
Will my crown be
a crumbling crest;
Will my dwelling be
a feeble nest?

Outro

41.

The king's fall

The king have sinned,
On a thousandth chance.
The birds have seen,
He failed the test—
They dare wont sing.
His basest thoughts—
He manifests,
When he list expects.
He fell from the top
At the seventh sense.
He's proudly dressed—
The land is cursed;
The high empress,
Is not impressed.
The public seem:
To lose interest,
The time he gets,
He poorly spends.
Every lie ever told—
He understands.
The slaves agree;
They have to flee—
His promises—
He fails to keep
The prince, will inherit,
The kingdom no more.
He won't obey
No preserving law.
They shall go against

The LORD's plans,
For he took his hand away
From the entire clan.
Now the prince can binge,
And use savage slang.
Their hearts shall go
After trivial things—
Grandparents to offspring's.

42.

Who are we to judge

When we come to conclude—
To say there is nothing wrong but all is just is,
Lead by greed—to acts of injustice.
Who are we to skip the scriptures
If we fail to practice;
To take constructive criticism for offences;
Who are we to live lies and lough at repentance—
Feeding the five of our senses
based on hunch and swinging moods.
Apart from the inner truth.

Who are we to conclude
That there is nothing bad,
And nothing good.
Based on shifting moods.
With planks in our own eyes—
Sporting specs of saw dust,
From the eyes of the just—
Holding our heart's broken parts
And trauma scars,
We feel in charge,
To spot the wrong and right,
Without the inner light.

Who are we to slaughter
the livestock, just to feed—
and still feel worthy to live.
When we forgive—
Who are we to hold a grudge,
at first place;
And to be followed to fate by false faith.
Who are we to differ,
without a reason or question;

To throw fires—without backfire expectations;
Lacking the truth—to blindly conclude, on a first impression.
Too proud to be wronged and to take blames for our actions;
Denying love, for lust, and self-gratification.

43.

After pride

The master:
Every after pride was a massive fall;
Every boastful start ended really small;
Every transgression built a burrier wall;
Every brag about tomorrow
Ended in some form of sorrow
Why then be proud and not expect a fall to follow;
You persist in sin and expect to stay fly—
Hence the space is the spy full of eyes.
If pride caught you when it calls
Why not prepare for a fall—

The scholar:
Now that we saw for sure—
After every pride—comes a fall
I'm watching my mind—purging
Every proud thought,
Before the remnants that remains—subside.
Till there is no more proud thought to hide—
Now that a fall is no more surprise.

44.

"Be"

Rise you are the chosen;
Be like the waves of the ocean in motion,
With courage and caution.
In rage and distortions—
Be the sheltering potion;
In heart be open—
True and outspoken;
With the word to mend the hearts broken.
Be all this and more,
Remaining meek
And slaves to the law.

Break the curses recurring in cycles;
Rise to the livity of ital.
Grateful for the little that seedless in season.
Be the sacred temple—upon which the Holy Ghost dwells;
Travel through times and foretell—
The gospel.
Be the best you can still be—for life is indeed brief.
Grateful for the sun and the air we do breathe—.
Beyond pleasure's greed—find your true needs,
And let the LORD lead.

Be the kind God sends—
To set the nations free;
In the land—be the change you want to see;
In season—a fruit bearing tree;
In chaos—seek your inner peace.
Be meek, kind, and mentally free—
The long searched missing puzzle piece
To fix the master piece

Be tender like a child, in heart,

And play your part—set apart.
Be like Nike and just do it despite
the way it seems by sight.
Determined to rise above the limits of the sky—
Be satisfied with the LORD's supply
And make it multiply.

45.

My worth

What is the worth of my words
If I speak—without being spirit led,
What value can they hold,
If my soul is junk fed
What is the worth of my words
If my pen is still red
What is the worth of my truth
If it's never out—read.
What is the worth of my words
If the only glots I grasp
Are the glots I found here on earth—
In my arrival through a typical birth—
Into the very flesh that counts down to death.
How profound—how strong
Can be—my own sung songs,
If every sound is from the source?
How good are my scrawls,
If I never designed a letter
Or a font?
How fair is my tone,
If I have no language of my own.
How fair is my satire
If I never set the heart into the fire
that inspires.
What uploads does anyone owe,
for my entrusted chores.
What's my worth if not I—
But The most high—who sent the Messiah.
In my heart's desires,
What if im possesed by the spirit of the prophet Isaiah.
What's the worth of my works
If I'm Gods own art work—love inspired.

About the Author

LUFUNO ROMEO MANWADU IS a mystical-poet, born on a Monday afternoon, the 29th of October, 1990, in a rustic village of South Africa's Northern Province—on the edge of disorder, scarcity, and crime. From as early as age nine, long before he understood what poetry was, Lufuno found relief in pouring his heart onto paper and singing out his inner world. What began as songs of hope, love, and liberation eventually evolved into the spiritual and visionary poetry he now offers the world.

A poetic soul with a deep hunger for introspection, transformation, and divine expression, Manwadu writes from the intersection of pain and purpose, of earthly truth and eternal fire. He is not merely a writer; he is an initiator—a sacred scribe crafting spiritual passages where souls ascend toward God-like wisdom. Drawing inspiration from The holy-ghost fire, Scripture, his vivid imagination, and the raw beauty of daily life.

Though he also writes in Tshivenda, his mother tongue, Manwadu chooses to write predominantly in English. Not out of disloyalty to his roots, but out of a longing to reach and be understood by as many of his earthly beloveds as possible. He believes translated poetry is often stripped of its original essence—its satire, tone, and poetic figure—and so he set himself the task of mastering English as a direct vehicle of expression. The result is poetry that is rich with internal and external rhyme, spiritual satire, and both classic and self-invented poetic figures, always rooted in real-life matters and existential truths.

Manwadu holds a 3-year Diploma in Public Administration and Management from UNISA, which he credits for helping him learn to articulate deep thoughts due to the long essays he had to write there. He is currently aspiring studies in Performing Arts to further nourish his passion academically and professionally.

His work thrives on rhythm, rhyme, and alliteration, yet it pulses with something rarer: spiritual urgency, divine fire, and a prophetic edge. From metaphysical meditations to the pain of human suffering, his poetry often carries the bold message that—*it is time to wake up, heal, and create alongside God.*

A vegan activist and natural minimalist, Lufuno has always shown an acute sensitivity to colors, sounds, and patterns—traits often misunderstood as "too picky" or "too realistic." Yet he regards this sensitivity not as a flaw, but as a God-intended trait, a divine mechanism for spiritual discernment and artistic precision. Whether through music, clothing, food, or poetry, this spiritual selectivity deepens his self-expression and connection to divine creativity, much like a form of natural selection within the human mind.

He believes that true poetry comes from the same source as true prophecy and healing music—from the mind of God, waiting to be tapped by any soul willing to contain the Holy Spirit's flame. According to Manwadu, natural poetry flows not only from talent, but from how deeply one can attune to divine frequencies and expand the capacity to hold fire, without being consumed.

Though deeply introspective and often quiet in speech, he is a fervent seeker of truth. His writing reflects a relentless curiosity—existential questions, spiritual awakenings, and raw revelations permeate his verse. A lover of constructive critique over empty praise, he believes flattery is a hindrance to growth and that truth, even when uncomfortable, is more edifying than applause.

The Dream We Call Reality is not simply a debut poetry book—it is a sacred threshold into a world of higher perception. It is a cry, a call, a prayer, and a mirror. And it introduces Lufuno Romeo Manwadu not just as a poet, but as a watchman with a pen, a mystic of the page, and a spiritual craftsman bearing witness to eternity.